A First Look at Art

Creatures

Ruth Thomson

CHELSEA CLUBHOUSE
An Imprint of Chelsea House Publishers
A Haights Cross Communications Company
Philadelphia

This edition first published in 2004 in the United States of America by Chelsea Clubhouse, a division of Chelsea House Publishers and a subsidiary of Haights Cross Communications.

A Haights Cross Communications Company

Chelsea Clubhouse
1974 Sproul Road, Suite 400
Broomall, PA 19008-0914
www.chelseahouse.com

Library of Congress Cataloging-in-Publication Data applied for. ISBN 0-7910-7945-7

First published in the UK in 2003 by
Chrysalis Children's Books
The Chrysalis Building, Bramley Road,
London W10 6SP

Copyright © Chrysalis Children's Books, an imprint of Chrysalis Books Group, plc 2003
Text Copyright © Ruth Thomson 2003
Illustrator: Linda Francis
Photographer: Steve Shott
Consultant: Erika Langmuir, formerly head of education at the National Gallery, London

The author and publishers would like to thank the following people for their contributions to this book: Liz Burton, Clare Whyles, Saskia Van der Zee and their pupils.

Printed in China

Picture acknowledgements

Front cover: Estate of Eileen Agar; 4: Philadelphia Museum of Art, Bequest of Lisa Norris Elkins; 5: Bridgeman Art Library; 6: Bridgeman Art Library/© ADAGP, Paris and DACS, London 2003; 6: Bridgeman Art Library/© Succession Picasso/DACS; 10: Estate of Eileen Agar; 15: Gift of Mr and Mrs Klaus G Perls, © 2003 Board of Trustees, National Gallery of Art Washington/ARS, NY and DACS, London 2003; 18/19: AKG London/National Gallery of Art, Washington; 22/23: Gift of Mrs Richard E Danielson and Mrs Chauncey McCormick, 1933.786, reproduction, The Art Institute of Chicago; 26/27: AKG London/Albright-Knox Art Gallery, Buffalo (NY)/© Succession Miro, DACS, 2003.

Contents

ANIMALS IN ART

Creatures, both real and imaginary, have always fascinated artists. In this book we'll see how rich and varied animal artwork can be. We'll explore some of the different ways in which artists have portrayed animals. You can find out what inspired the artists and learn about their techniques. There are also questions to help you look at the works in detail and ideas for creating your own pictures and sculptures.

⊙ You'll find answers to the questions and information about the artists on pages 30-31.

Arty Tips

✫ Look for Arty Tips boxes that suggest handy techniques and materials to use in your own work.

Picture Hunt

✫ Picture Hunt boxes suggest other artists and artworks that you might like to find.

Lascaux cave painting (unknown artist)
Dordogne, France, c15,000 BC

Introducing animals

Some of the first pictures ever made were of animals. Stone Age artists painted lively images of cows, horses, bison, and deer on the walls of dark caves. They used colors made by mixing together powdered rocks and plants with clay and water.

Noah's Ark
Edward Hicks
1846 (26.3 x 30.4 inches)

Telling tales

Animal paintings often tell us stories. This one illustrates a scene from the Bible, when creatures fled in pairs to the ark to escape the coming flood.

Some artists in ancient civilizations painted imaginary creatures that were described in their myths. Others used real animals as symbols to give meaning to artwork. Bulls and lions, for example, represented strength and power.

Animal artists

Throughout history, many forms of animal art have developed. Some artists have been with explorers to distant countries, painting and drawing the wildlife they've seen. Some have painted animal scenes to hang on the walls of people's homes. Other artists have made their living painting portraits or creating sculptures of people's favorite pets.

TEXTURE AND MOOD

The Cat
Tsuguharu Foujita
1927
(15 x 18.1 inches)

The way something feels to the touch is called **texture**. Artists can suggest textures by using lines, shapes, and light and dark tones.

Lines can be fine or heavy, solid or broken. Shapes can be curvy or jagged. The use of light and dark tones may suggest shine, softness, sharpness, or roughness.

Soft and furry

The body of this pet cat was drawn with lots of short lines. These suggest the soft texture of fur. The lines are gently blended with a thin layer, or **wash**, of ink.

◉ Which parts of the cat are drawn with a *solid* line?

◉ How would these parts feel compared with the rest?

Cat and Bird
Pablo Picasso
1939
(38.2 x 51.2
inches)

Sharp and scary

This cat's bold, solid outline makes it look tense and alert. Its back is arched, its tail is stiff and upright, and its front leg sticks out at a sharp angle.

Picasso liked street cats because they are cunning, skillful hunters. His painting shows how fierce and fearless these animals can be.

Picasso used blocks of solid color, which add to the aggressive feel of the painting.

◉ Which parts of this cat make it look fierce?

◉ How has Picasso emphasized that cats have keen eyesight?

◉ If you could touch the cats in these two pictures, how would they feel? Think of three words to describe each one.

7

MAKING MARKS

Lines and textures

Practice making different kinds of marks using soft **pastels**, colored pencils, and felt-tips. Make long, flowing marks; scratchy scribbles; strong, crisp lines; and short, soft ones.

Cat surprise!

◉ Fold a sheet of paper as shown below.

◉ Decide whether the cat inside will be fierce or friendly. On the outer flaps, draw some textured marks that give clues about its character.

Joel, age 8

Andrew, age 8

Zahra, age 8

◉ Inside, draw the cat, again using marks that suggest its personality.

Joel, age 8

Andrew, age 8

Zahra, age 8

Arty Tips

✬ Use pastels and pencils with soft lead for making soft, smudgy textures.

✬ Use rollerball pens, colored pencils, and pencils with hard lead for making sharper, more precise marks.

8

Two-faced cats

⊙ Draw the outline of a cat's head on stiff paper, and cut it out.

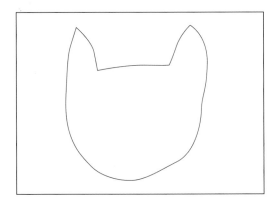

⊙ Trace this head onto another piece of stiff paper to create a second, identical outline.

⊙ Cut this out.

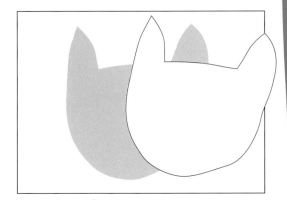

⊙ Use paints, felt-tips or crayons to create one friendly and one fierce cat face.

Inez, age 8

⊙ Use soft colors and smudgy marks for the friendly cat.

Daniel, age 8

David, age 9

friendly

Eleri, age 8

⊙ Use bold outlines and strong colors for the fierce cat.

Zamir, age 8

fierce

Aubrey, age 8

Aaron, age 9

⊙ Glue the two faces back to back with a popsicle stick between them.

Picture Hunt

☆ Many other artists, such as Théodore Géricault, Paul Klee, Franz Marc, and Pierre Auguste Renoir, painted cats. Find some of their images of cats and decide whether these artists saw cats as soft, gentle pets or as wild, aggressive animals.

NATURE'S PATTERNS

Artists often create pictures to express ideas that interest them. Eileen Agar was intrigued by the way new life begins and changes from one stage to another.

In this work, she explores how a bird develops. It grows inside an egg until it is ready to hatch. Then tap, tap, tap! The bird cracks the eggshell and pops out. Once it is old enough, the bird may lay new eggs of its own.

Bird beginnings

This colorful bird stands out on the page. Its clear, crisp form is as flat as a cardboard cut-out.

Agar overlapped two large egg forms with the bird to show how eggs become birds and birds, in their turn, lay eggs. The egg on the left looks cracked.

Maybe the bird has come out of the cracked egg. Or is it still waiting to hatch inside the other one?

◉ Can you *see* any other hints of egg shapes?

Playful patterns

Agar filled her picture with different patterns. Some of them remind us of feathers. Others look like broken eggshells or nesting twigs.

◉ Can you *spot* all these patterns? What part of a bird do they remind you of?
- zig-zags
- circles
- checks
- stripes
- chevrons (V shapes)
- irregular spots

◉ Find colors that are repeated on different parts of the bird and some that are used only once. How has Agar made the bird stand out?

The Bird
Eileen Agar
1969
(40.2 x 50.4 inches)

DECORATIVE DISPLAYS

Pattern practice

◉ Fold a square piece of paper four times to make sixteen little squares.

◉ Draw a different pattern inside each square. Use your ideas to decorate a bird.

A beautiful bird

◉ Draw a bird shape on white paper, and cut it out.

◉ Cover the bird with patterns, using felt-tip pens or paints.

◉ Glue the bird onto a contrasting colored background, to make it really stand out.

◉ Add some extra decorative details all around the bird.

Picture Hunt

✧ Compare Agar's work with pictures by other artists, such as Gustave Klimt, Henri Matisse, and Sonia Delauney-Terk, who often use a great many patterns.

✧ Look at works by M. C. Escher, who often changed one shape, such as a fish, into another, such as a bird.

Emily, Suzie, Flora, Zak, and Martha, all age 8

A hatching egg

◉ Draw an egg shape and a bird shape on stiff paper. Cut them out.

◉ Cut the egg in half, using a jagged line. Stick colorful pieces of paper all over both halves. Then glue the two halves onto a colored background, leaving room for the bird.

◉ Cover the bird with pieces torn from newspaper or magazine pages. Stick the bird onto the page, as if it is hatching from the egg.

Zahra, Rowan, Alex, Lottie, Luke, Andrew, George, and Aonghus, all age 8

Eggcellent ornaments

◉ Ask an adult to help you hard-boil some eggs.

◉ When the eggs are completely cool and dry, paint them all over with bright patterns (see Arty Tips).

Natasha, Hannah,
Grace, Helen, James, and Josh, all age 9

Arty Tips

✬ It's easiest if you paint one end of your egg, then let it dry before painting the other end. That way you can always hold the egg without smudging any paint.

✬ You can use almost any kind of paint. When it's dry, add a coat of varnish for extra shine. You could also try painting your egg with clear glue and rolling it in glitter.

✬ Hard-boiled eggs won't last forever. For a more permanent ornament, use a smooth pebble or modeling clay.

CREATURES IN MOTION

**Oval Dish
with Fish
and Reptiles**
French School (imitation
of Bernard Palissy pottery)
19th century (15 x 18.5 inches)

Animals may slither, slink, or squirm. Some twist, twirl, or twitch. Others wriggle, creep, crawl, gallop, or glide. Artists can capture movements like these in different ways.

A pond on a plate

The bodies and tails of the creatures on this pottery plate bend, curve, and curl this way and that, to suggest that they have been caught mid-action.

The potter has arranged the animals carefully, so that they don't touch or overlap one another.

◉ Think of words to describe the way each of these creatures might move:
- the snake
- the frog and toad
- the fish
- the lizards
- the crayfish

Swimming in the air

This fish sculpture *really* moves. It hangs from the ceiling on a wire and swings gently to and fro in the faintest breeze. Moving sculptures like this are called mobiles. They were invented by Alexander Calder, who made this fish.

Shapes and scales

Notice how Calder bent strong wire into the outline of a fish. He used thin wire to make a network of scale shapes and tied on dangling bits and pieces. As the objects twirl, they catch the light and glisten and shimmer.

Bits and pieces

Calder used all sorts of shiny objects for the fish scales.

⊚ See if you can spot:
- a key
- metal strainers
- pieces of mirror
- a metal funnel
- colored glass fragments
- pottery pieces
- spiral shapes
- colored wire

⊚ Imagine seeing the fish on a sunny day. Which bits and pieces would glint and sparkle?

Finny Fish
Alexander Calder
1948 (26 x 60 inches)

MODELING MOVEMENT

A watery world

Transform a paper plate or plastic tray into a mini world, filled with wildlife.

◉ Paint the plate blue, with streaky ripples.

◉ Make wiggling fish, a thrashing squid, a flapping turtle, and other moving creatures from colored modeling clay.

Farhaan, age 9, and Mahliqa, age 8

Dan and Nancy-Luz,
both age 8

◉ Arrange the creatures on the plate or tray.

◉ Glue on some real seashells.

◉ You might like to add some green raffia seaweed, as well.

◉ For a shimmery water effect, cover the tray or plate with plastic wrap or clear cellophane.

Arty Tips

✦ If you want to suggest that the creatures are moving, show them with one or more raised legs, waving antennae, or a twisting or curved body.

Marvelous mobiles

◉ Make your own mobile by twisting together pieces of thin garden wire.

◉ Thread on shiny beads, tinsel balls, or sparkly sequins as you construct your creature, or attach feathers, pipe cleaners, and pieces of shiny paper once the creature is complete.

Luke, age 8, and Harry, age 9

Yasmine, age 8

◉ Hang your mobile somewhere where it can catch the light and turn in the breeze.

Tristan, age 8

Sculpture Hunt

✿ Look for pictures of other mobiles made by Calder. Many are made up of simple, brightly colored shapes that hang from different "arms," at varying heights.

✿ Find out about the works of Jean Tinguely, who also made moving sculptures from everyday objects.

COLOR AND CAMOUFLAGE

Wild animals are good at hiding. They lurk among leaves and bend around branches. Artists can play with **camouflage** to create surprises. Beware!

⊙ What can you *see* hiding here? What might you hear?

⊙ If you were in this forest, where and how would you hide?

The colors

Rousseau used many shades of green when he painted this forest. The pale green and yellow in the background make it seem hot and steamy.

The colors of the animals help them to hide. They sometimes blend in with the leaves and flowers.

⊙ How many different greens can you find?

⊙ Can you *see* colors that match animals to plants?

Leaves and flowers

Notice how every leaf and flower is crisply painted and clearly separate from the others next to it.

◉ How many differently shaped leaves and flowers can you spot?

Inspirations

Rousseau painted many tropical scenes like this one. He claimed that he had visited tropical forests when he was with the French army in Mexico. This was not true. In fact, he imagined them, using photos and books as reference. He also spent a great deal of time sketching tropical plants and wild animals at the plant gardens in Paris.

◉ What is odd about the two monkeys in the foreground of this imaginary scene?

Tropical Forest with Monkeys
Henri Rousseau
1910 (51 x 64 inches)

19

IN THE WILD

Complete the animal

◉ Cut out one important detail of an animal, such as its nose, teeth, scales, or ears, from a magazine photograph.

◉ Glue it onto a piece of paper.

◉ Paint the rest of the animal around it.

◉ Include a background that shows where the animal lives.

Maddy, age 8

Martha, age 8

A monkey mask

◉ Cut a circle out of stiff paper or use a paper plate to make the face.

◉ Glue on crumpled balls of newspaper for a nose, cheeks, and brow.

◉ Put several layers of newspaper strips, dipped in papier-mâché paste, over the face. Leave it to dry.

◉ Paint the face with monkey features. Glue on some wooly fur.

◉ Make separate paper ears, and staple these to the monkey's head.

Kieran, age 9

Picture Hunt

✦ Find other rain forest pictures by Rousseau, such as Virgin Forest at Sunset, The Dream, The Snake Charmer, and Tiger in a Tropical Storm (Surprised!).

✦ Compare Rousseau's tropical forest picture with woodland paintings by Charles Burchfield, Emily Carr, or Gustav Klimt.

Color mixing

Make several different greens.

◉ Mix together equal amounts of blue and yellow.

◉ Mix more blue than yellow.

◉ Mix more yellow than blue.

◉ Add a little white to your mixtures to make lighter **tints**.

◉ Add a little black or red to make darker shades.

A green jungle

◉ Use all the greens you have mixed to make a lush rain forest picture.

◉ Include some brightly colored animals, snakes, and birds that stand out against the leafy background.

George, age 9, and Aaron, age 8

Joseph, age 9, and Tristan, age 8

A camouflage collage

◉ Make a rain forest **collage**, using strips of torn paper, crumpled tissue, and corrugated cardboard.

◉ Hide some animals and birds among the leaves, in the water, or under fallen branches.

Saint George Killing the Dragon
Bernardo Martorell
1430/35
(61.1 x 38.6 inches)

Some creatures, such as dragons, do not exist in real life. But artists often make them up out of various parts of real animals, such as mammals, birds, and reptiles.

◉ What animals has this artist used for the head, body, tail, wings, and feet of his dragon?

The tale of Saint George

This picture tells the story of a dragon who terrorized a kingdom. To keep it away, people gave it sheep to eat. When there were no sheep left, people drew lots each day to decide who would be the dragon's next victim. One day the princess drew the lot. But in the nick of time, Saint George rode by and killed the dragon.

◉ Notice how the artist has included all details of the story. Look for:

• the worried people in the kingdom
• a sheep and the princess
• skulls and bones of victims
• the dragon and his cave
• Saint George

MAKING MONSTERS

A monster poster

◉ Paint a detailed picture of a monster in eye-catching colors.

◉ Glue the picture onto a larger piece of colored paper, and draw a frame around it.

◉ Write **WANTED** in big letters at the top of the paper.

Picture Hunt

✦ Try to find pictures of other strange beasts made up of a mixture of animals. Search for a centaur, griffin, chimera, cockatrice, hippogriff, or amphisbaena. (Look them up in a dictionary first.)

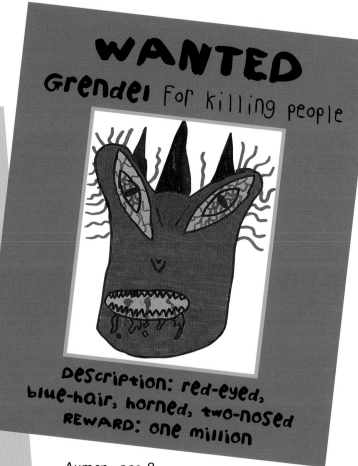

WANTED
Grendel for killing people

DESCRIPTION: red-eyed, blue-hair, horned, two-nosed
REWARD: one million

Aymen, age 8

WANTED
Grendel for murder! Terrorizing! cannibalism! Attacks!

DESCRIPTION: huge, mean, slimy, many-eyed
REWARD: bag of gold

Keeley, age 9

◉ Give the monster's name.

◉ Say why it is wanted.

◉ Under its picture, describe the monster's main features.

◉ Offer a big reward!

Monster mix

◉ Draw a sketch of a monster made up from parts of several real animals. Think about the useful features of different animals — such as their wings, teeth, feet, and necks.

◉ Think of answers to these questions about your monster. Include some of these details in your work:

● How does it move? Can it fly, swim, jump, or run?

Daniel, age 9

Luc, age 8, and Jack and Joseph, both age 9

● Where does it live — in the sea, inside a volcano, on a mountaintop, in the desert, or in a cave?

● What does it eat — plants, people, or other animals?

● Is it colorful? Does it have any patterning or texture?

Arty Tips

✰ To make a monster look really scary, exaggerate the size of its eyes, teeth, claws, or horns.

✰ To emphasize a monster's strength, size, or a particular ability, make its head, neck, body, wings, or legs stand out.

Eleri and Ellie, both age 8

IMAGINARY CREATURES

Artists can paint whatever creatures they can imagine. Miró said that staring at cracks in his walls helped give him ideas for these fantastic creatures.

Party time

The Harlequin (the figure with a blue and red face) is having a noisy party with some unusual guests.

◉ Discover:
• a bird with a bow and arrow body
• three or more floating creatures
• two or more winged creatures
• a red-faced cat
• creatures with flower heads
◉ What other creatures can you find?

The Harlequin's Carnival
Joan Miró
1924-25 (26 x 36.6 inches)

A carnival dance

The picture is filled with lively music and dancing.

Spot the musician with his guitar, some musical notes, and a large ear listening from the ladder.

Notice how the shapes of the creatures suggest different movements.

◉ Which creatures sway, wiggle, or bounce to the music?

The colors

The party is in a bare room. The plain wall and floor make the colorful creatures stand out.

Miró makes the same shades of blue, red, and yellow dance rhythmically across the picture.

JUST IMAGINE

Blotty creatures

◉ Fold a piece of paper in half and make a crease along the fold. Open the paper out again.

◉ Put several different colored blobs of paint on one half of the paper.

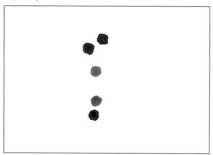

◉ Fold the paper in half again. Rub it, so that the blobs inside squish onto both sides of the paper. Open the paper, and let the paint dry.

◉ What sort of creature do the blots suggest to you? Use a pen, felt-tips, or paint to transform the blots into a strange animal.

Louise, age 9

Natasha, age 9

Rowan, age 8

◉ Use colored modeling clay to make some strange creatures, and create your own party or parade.

◉ Will your creatures have one eye, lots of eyes, or none at all?

◉ Will they have feet or tails, or will they wobble about on a round base?

◉ Will they have arms, paws, or wings, or none of these?

◉ Will they be plainly colored, striped, or patterned?

Picture Hunt

✦ Make a collection of paintings or drawings of imaginary creatures by other 20th-century artists, such as Max Ernst, Paul Klee, and Mervyn Peake.

Joe, age 9

Imran, age 9

Holly, age 8

Amy, age 8

Leo, age 8

Dan, age 9

David, age 9

◉ Give each creature a name and make up a story about them.

ARTISTS AND ANSWERS

ANIMALS IN ART (pages 4/5)

About the LASCAUX CAVES

The Lascaux caves were discovered in 1940 by four boys who were out walking. The cave walls are covered with nearly 600 paintings and engravings of animals, which date back to around 15,000 BC. Many are hunting scenes, typical of Stone Age times.

About EDWARD HICKS

Hicks (1780-1849) was a self-taught American artist, who began his career by painting coaches and signs. He was very religious and painted hundreds of pictures inspired by verses in the Bible.

TEXTURE AND MOOD (pages 6/7)

Answers for page 6

• The cat's ears, nose, mouth, and leg joint are all painted with a solid line.
• These parts would feel harder than its furry body.

About TSUGUHARU FOUJITA

Foujita (1886-1968) was born in Japan and studied art at the Imperial School for Fine Arts in Tokyo. In 1913, he moved to Paris to learn more from European artists. He traveled widely, especially in North and South America. His landscapes, portraits, and cats are painted in a delicate way, combining traditional Japanese and modern European styles. He also painted the walls of a chapel in Reims, in northern France.

Answers for page 7

• The sharp teeth, claws, and lined brow look fierce.
• Picasso emphasized the cat's eyes with several circles.
• Foujita's cat is soft, relaxed, and furry; Picasso's is angular, tense, and tight.

About PABLO PICASSO

Picasso (1886-1968) was probably the most famous artist of the 20th century. He was born in Spain, the son of an art teacher, and he showed a talent for art as a child. He studied in Barcelona and Madrid, then lived mainly in France. Picasso experimented with many ways of painting and sculpting. With his artist friend Georges Braque, he developed a new art style called **Cubism**. He made collages and sculptures from found objects, designed ballet sets, and made **etchings**. He painted pottery, made plaster models, and learned how to weld, cut, and fold metal to make sculptures.

NATURE'S PATTERNS (pages 10/11)

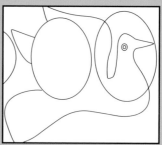

Answers for page 10

• There is a small blue egg under the curve of the bird's body. Parts of other eggs are hinted at elsewhere in the background.
• Zig-zags are on the eggs, the bird's neck and tail, and in the top background. The bird's eye is two circles. There are checks below the bird and stripes on the bird's head, wing tip, and tail. Chevrons are on the bird's chest and on one egg. There are green and pink irregular spots on the eggs.
• Red, very deep pink, deep pink, and strong orange are used only once. All the other colors are repeated. The bird stands out because it is painted in light, bright colors against a dark background.

About EILEEN AGAR

Agar (1899-1991) was a British artist. She was born in Buenos Aires in Argentina, but she moved with her family to England in 1911. She studied art in London and spent several years in Paris, where she was influenced by an art style called Surrealism. Surrealist artists were interested in dreams, chance, and the unconscious mind. Agar was also fascinated by nature, particularly the shapes of plants, shells, fossils, and eggs. Besides painting pictures, she created collages from found objects.

CREATURES IN MOTION (pages 14/15)

Answer for page 14

• Snakes wiggle, slither, slip, and slide; fish dive, twist, skim, and glide; crayfish crawl, wiggle, and swim; frogs and toads jump or leap; lizards slink, climb, dash, and scuttle.

About BERNARD PALISSY

Palissy (c1510-1590) – the artist who inspired this dish – was a French potter. Palissy made molds from real objects, such as shells and dead fish. He laid the shapes on dishes, which were then fired and glazed.

Answer for page 15

• The mirrors and glass would glisten and sparkle most in sunlight. There would also be reflections from the shiny metal and pottery parts.

About ALEXANDER CALDER

Calder (1898-1976) was an American who trained as an engineer before becoming a sculptor. His early works were wire portraits of celebrities, wire and wooden animals, and a moving miniature wire circus. In addition to inventing both hanging and standing mobiles, Calder made moving sculptures that were powered by either hand or motor. His later works were huge metal sculptures for public places.

COLOR AND CAMOUFLAGE (pages 18/19)

Answers for pages 18 and 19

• There are five monkeys and a snake hiding in the painting.
• There are at least seven different greens.
• Some monkeys match the yellow flowers. The gray snake and monkeys match branches.
• There are at least seven differently shaped leaves and two types of flowers.
• The monkeys are fishing with poles.

About HENRI ROUSSEAU

Rousseau (1844-1910) was a self-taught French painter. He served in the army and then worked as a customs officer in Paris. After he retired, he started painting portraits, scenes of everyday life and flowers, as well as imaginary, dream-like scenes set in exotic surroundings. Rousseau was admired by Picasso, who organized a banquet in his honor.

A MYTHICAL BEAST (pages 22/23)

Answer for page 23

• The dragon has the hairy head of a wolf, the scaly body and tail of a reptile, the wings of a bat, and the sharp claws of a bird of prey.

About BERNARDO MARTORELL

Martorell (c1400-1452) came from Spain and worked mainly in Barcelona. He is known for his painted altarpieces and **miniatures**.

IMAGINARY CREATURES (pages 26/27)

Answer for page 27

• The Harlequin, the floating creatures with long tails, and the faceless white creature are all swaying; the white snake-like creature is wiggling; the creatures on the floor and the springed creature in the air (top center) are bouncing.

About JOAN MIRÓ

Miró (1893-1983) – a Spanish artist – studied art in Barcelona. He then went to Paris and met Picasso, who helped him exhibit his work. Miró's early paintings were very detailed, based on things he saw, but often arranged oddly and painted in strange colors. Later his paintings became simpler and more dream-like. People, creatures, and objects are hinted at by odd shapes, and sometimes words or symbols are included. Miró also made brightly colored sculptures.

GLOSSARY

camouflage—blending in with your surroundings

collage—a picture made by sticking bits of paper, fabric, or other objects, onto a background

Cubism—a 20th-century art style, developed by Pablo Picasso and Georges Braque, in which artists broke down subjects into geometric shapes

etching—a form of print-making in which the artist scratches an image onto a metal plate, ink is worked into the scratched marks, and the plate is pressed onto paper to print

miniatures—very small, detailed paintings

pastels—soft crayons that can be chalky (soft pastels) or oily (oil pastels)

texture—how something feels to the touch, for example, rough or smooth

tints—light tones of a color, often made by adding white

wash—a layer of thin, watery paint or ink

INDEX